The World of Diaghilev

Christopher Wood: drawing of Serge Diaghilev with Bronislava Nijinska, Jean Cocteau, Darius Milhaud and Boris Kochno, 1924

John Percival

The World of

DIAGHILEV

HARMONY BOOKS
New York

Mikhail Larionov: caricatures of Diaghilev and his circle, about 1920
By courtesy of Sotheby & Co

Revised edition first published by
The Herbert Press Limited, 65 Belsize Lane, London NW3 5AU

Designed by Gillian Greenwood

Library of Congress Catalog Card Number: 79–63843
Printed in Great Britain
ISBN 0–517–539020
       0–517–539039 pbk

Contents

Pablo Picasso: drawing of Serge Diaghilev and his manager Salisburg, 1919

His impact

When Dima Filosofov's country cousin arrived in St Petersburg in the summer of 1890 his little circle of friends hardly knew what had hit them. Quite a lot of people subsequently had a similar experience on first encountering Serge Diaghilev. He showed his fellow-countrymen the glories of their own painting which they had previously overlooked or taken for granted. He brought Russian art and music to the west. He founded a new kind of ballet company that became, for the twenty years it existed, the most famous in the world. Even now, half a century after his death, his name has almost irresistible fascination.

Diaghilev cannot have been a very attractive man. He was a snob, with apparently unlimited faith in his own invariable rightness on any issue; he took pains to make himself liked by people who could be helpful, but acted ruthlessly towards any collaborator whose service he no longer wanted. Yet he could be overwhelmingly charming or generous and, while they worked with him, his dancers and other colleagues were well looked after.

He had an impressive appearance: big in build, with a head that was proportionately even bigger. He smiled with his mouth alone, the rest of his face remaining serious. He was aloof, superstitious, inclined to hypochondria—although as a diabetic he had some justification for that.

The first seasons of his ballet company succeeded because of the collection of outstanding soloists he was able to present and because of the unprecedented fervour of the more exotic works in the repertory. Later these soloists left one by one and his repertory changed its character, yet his success continued.

The effect of Diaghilev's Russian Ballet on public taste was sensational and far-reaching. Thanks to what they admired in his productions people dressed differently and adopted a different style of furnishing and decorating their homes. On a more long-term basis, other people had to change their way of presenting ballet (and opera too, to some extent), and his example inspired a major revival of the art of ballet in the west.

Today his legend lives on. People queued in the snow to see the Diaghilev exhibition organized by Richard Buckle in 1954 to commemorate the twenty-fifth anniversary of his death. Since then, sales at the Sotheby Parke Bernet salerooms in London and New York have repeatedly achieved staggering prices for designs, curtains and old costumes associated with Diaghilev. Competition to make a film about him and his most celebrated dancer Nijinsky has been almost equally keen. Those ballets of his company which are still danced today are still a draw: mention the names of most ballets to the ordinary man in the street and he will look at you blankly, but everyone has heard of *Les Sylphides* or *Petrushka*.

Diaghilev's story is pretty well documented, but a lot of myths and misunderstandings persist. I remember the man who reeled rather drunkenly up to a small crowd waiting outside Covent Garden very early one morning to buy ballet tickets. 'Did you ever see that Daggylev?' he demanded. 'He was the greatest dancer who ever lived.' There is something rather marvellous about a man who lives on in the popular memory like this, however wrong people are about him.

Serge Diaghilev, about 1909

His background

Serge Pavlovich Diaghilev was born in the Selistchev barracks, in the Novgorod province of Russia, on 19 March 1872. It was a difficult delivery and his mother died a few days later. His father, an army officer, married again after two years, and it was young Serge's stepmother, Elena, who was responsible for his upbringing. At first this was in St Petersburg, but when the boy was ten the Diaghilevs moved because of debt to live in the family mansion at Perm.

The family was well off (Serge's father inherited the family estate and distilleries) and they lived in a style that encouraged love of the arts. There were musical evenings when chamber music, songs and sometimes whole operas were performed. Books and pictures abounded.

The boy inherited the typical Diaghilev appearance: the thick-set build, deep sad eyes, protruding jaw and plump, fleshy underlip. The mixture of enthusiasm and stubbornness which characterized all his activities was also common in the family.

9

At eighteen he matriculated from high school and was sent to St Petersburg to enter university, to study law (a socially acceptable and not too demanding subject). He arrived in the summer of 1890 and stayed with his cousin Dima Filosofov, by whom he was introduced into a small band of friends already deeply interested in the arts and full of creative ambitions. The unofficial leader of the group was Alexander Benois, and Leon Bakst had been introduced into their circle only a few months before Diaghilev.

This was before any of the circle had made their name, but they were already full of ideas for advancement. At first they found the country cousin boorish and provincial, but he soon developed into a 'terrible fop', assiduous in doing the right thing socially, although still sometimes putting on a show of 'barbarism' when he thought it would serve his purpose.

The circle introduced Diaghilev to new trends in the arts, his main interest at first being music—he studied at the Conservatoire while still a law student. His aspirations to be a composer were ridiculed, however, first by Rimsky-Korsakov, to whom he went for advice, and then by his friends, when he played to them his own setting of the fountain scene from *Boris Godunov*. After this, Diaghilev became much more interested in painting, which had previously seemed not to attract him.

Opposite: Boris Kustodiev: portrait of Leon Bakst, 1910

Leon Bakst: portrait of Alexander Benois, about 1895

Having inherited some money he began to buy pictures. At first, according to Benois, his taste was erratic, but it developed rapidly. In 1895 he made, alone, a protracted tour of western Europe (he had previously been twice on pleasure trips with his cousin) specifically to fill in the gaps in his artistic knowledge. He obtained letters of introduction and was tireless in seeking out celebrities; by now he was in fact rather a snob, but he was able to make people like him when he tried, and many of the connexions he made at this time were invaluable in his later ventures.

By 1896 the group of friends were beginning to make their names—individually so far. It was about this time that Diaghilev first began to show an interest in ballet; he also published a couple of articles of art criticism in the newspaper *Novosti*. Benois dated the growth of Diaghilev's real ambition from these articles: 'As soon as he felt he had the power of influencing people and experienced the rapture of talking to the masses, Diaghilev became and remained a promoter, a man who had a definite mission in life.'

Diaghilev himself, in a letter to his stepmother, put it a little differently:

I am first a great charlatan, though with brio; secondly a great *charmeur*; thirdly, I have any amount of cheek; fourthly, I am a man with a great quantity of logic, but with very few principles; fifthly, I think I have no real gifts. All the same, I think I have just found my true vocation—being a Maecenas. I have all that is necessary save the money—*mais ça viendra*.

And come it did.

His first step was to organize an exhibition of German and English watercolours in 1887—a modest collection, apparently, but attracting attention by the originality and imagination with which the display was arranged. This led to backing for more ambitious projects: an exhibition of Scandinavian art, one combining Finnish and young Russian painters, and later another international show which introduced French impressionism to the Russian public. In 1898, too, Princess M. K. Tenishev and the manufacturer Slava Mamontov were persuaded to provide the financial backing for a new magazine *The World of Art* with Diaghilev as editor. Propagandist and didactic in tone, this was a serious review of painting, the applied arts, theatre, music and literature, in which most of Diaghilev's circle of friends participated. At last they had a platform for their views; to encourage modern movements and reveal to Russians the richness of their own art. But they were not interested only in ideas—they also went to great trouble to obtain improved typefaces, paper and printing blocks for the illustrations, so that the magazine became a thing of beauty on its own account.

Something of the same sort happened when Prince Sergei Wolkonsky was appointed director of the Imperial Theatres in 1899, a man young for such a post and sympathetic to the ideas of the *World of Art* circle, who engaged several of the painters to design new productions and also appointed Diaghilev 'for special missions'. One of these was editing the annual of the Imperial Theatres, which he transformed from a useful but dull record to a lavish illustrated volume. Even this commendable feat attracted some criticism, however, because he overran his budget.

Further criticism was provoked by Diaghilev's overbearing and tactless manner, and also by his private life. Although at that time Diaghilev denied homosexuality, spiteful rumours were passing and he even received a powder puff as an anonymous gift. Wolkonsky warned him to be discreet; but apparently without success. When Diaghilev was chosen to supervise production of Delibes' ballet *Sylvia*, permanent officials of the theatre protested at the infringement of their positions. The invitation to Diaghilev was withdrawn; the latter at once resigned from the editorship of the annual. A crisis blew up, thanks to the way everybody involved stood on their dignity; Diaghilev tried to pull strings to get the Emperor's support but instead was dismissed from his official attachment in terms which ruled out any further appointment, although he later succeeded in regaining the Tsar's favour.

With another change of director at the Imperial Theatres, some of Diaghilev's colleagues were given further commissions, in spite of attacks by *The World of Art* on the new director, Teliakovsky. Bakst especially had a great success designing the ballet *The Fairy Doll*. Diaghilev meanwhile (perhaps inspired by the success of a smaller similar show arranged by Benois) began preparation for a big historical exhibition of Russian portraits. He spent almost the whole of 1904 travelling about Russia for exhibits, and his lack of further interest in the magazine was one of the motives for closing it down that year.

The success of this 1905 exhibition, held under imperial patronage in the Tauride Palace at St Petersburg, made it possible for Diaghilev to obtain support for a further big exhibition of Russian art the following year in Paris. The Tsar lent priceless works from imperial collections, which encouraged other lenders. Many modern works by members of the *World of Art* group were shown too. The arrangement of the show in the Grand Palais was imaginative: Bakst created a small wooded garden as background for the sculptures, the ikons were hung on brocade-covered walls and the halls were decorated and furnished in the taste of the period shown in each. Later the exhibition was transported to Berlin and (in reduced form) Vienna.

His success at 'exporting' Russian painting led Diaghilev to experiment with organizing a concert in Paris at the Palais des Champs-Elysées, followed the next spring (1907) by a series of concerts at the Paris Opéra. Glazunov, Rachmaninov and Rimsky-Korsakov came to conduct their own works; Nikisch was the star among the other conductors; operatic excerpts were included with Chaliapin among the singers. As with the art exhibition, the printed programmes provided a lavishly illustrated and informative introduction.

Chaliapin's triumph (this was the beginning of the singer's world renown) led to the idea in 1908 of showing a complete Russian opera in Paris. Moussorgsky's *Boris Godunov* was chosen, but Diaghilev, already very conscious of dramatic effect as the highest criterion, insisted on changing the order of scenes, having some reorchestrated, restoring some traditional cuts in the music but making others. He even introduced (the idea was Benois') a monologue from Pushkin's poem on the same subject. The settings and costumes were elaborate; the story was that Diaghilev and Benois bought up all the eighteenth-century gold-embroidered neckerchiefs they could in the

Fedor Chaliapin as Boris in
Boris Godunov

Petersburg rag market to be cut up to make collars for the boyars (a rather wasteful procedure if true, but good publicity). The resulting production was immensely admired for the realism of its staging, for the chorus singing and for Chaliapin's tremendously dramatic interpretation of the title part.

Inevitably there had to be another opera season in Paris the next year, and this time Benois suggested taking ballet also, urging that the art had almost died out in the west, and would therefore be a novelty to its audiences; besides which Russia happened to have some exceptionally able young dancers at that time and a promising new choreographer, Michel Fokine. Benois was not entirely unbiased—he had collaborated with Fokine on a ballet, *Le Pavillon d'Armide*, for the Imperial Theatre in 1907; but eventually Diaghilev agreed to add one programme of three short ballets to his intended operatic repertory of Rimsky-Korsakov's *The Maid of Pskov* (which he renamed *Ivan the Terrible*), Borodin's *Prince Igor*, Glinka's *Ruslan and Ludmila*, Serov's *Judith* and a revival of *Boris*. During rehearsals, however, Diaghilev's patron the Grand Duke Vladimir (the Tsar's uncle) died and the ballerina Kchessinskaya (mistress formerly of the Tsar, and later of his cousin the Grand Duke André), who was to have taken part in the season, quarrelled with Diaghilev, possibly because she thought her role too small. The loss of this influential support led to the withdrawal of a promised

Fedor Chaliapin as Boris in
Boris Godunov

Fedor Chaliapin as Ivan in *Ivan the Terrible*

subsidy and even the use of the theatre for rehearsals was suddenly refused.

This blow made it necessary to cut back drastically, although Diaghilev managed to raise enough private support to avoid cancelling the season. He decided to present only one full opera, *Ivan the Terrible*, and one act apiece from *Igor* and *Ruslan*, each of these to be given on a programme with two ballets.

It had already been decided to show *Le Pavillon d'Armide* and two other existing ballets by Fokine, *Chopiniana* and *An Egyptian Night*. All of them underwent some changes at Diaghilev's insistence, including a new title for the Chopin ballet—which thus won immortality as *Les Sylphides*—and a revised story, designs (by Bakst), score and title (*Cleopatra*) for the Egyptian ballet. For this, some of the music by Arensky was replaced by Diaghilev with compositions from operas by Glinka, Moussorgsky, Rimsky-Korsakov and Taneyev, plus a bacchanale from Glazunov's ballet *The Seasons* and a new finale written by Tcherepnin. Only Diaghilev's old friend Valetchka Nouvel, it seems, thought there was anything odd about using such a Russian salad of a score; even Fokine's only objection was that 'It will be a new ballet.'

Nikolai Roerich: design for scene 2, *Ivan the Terrible*, 1909

Konstantin Korovin: design for act 1, *Ruslan and Ludmila*, 1909

Fokine also had the job of arranging the dances for *Prince Igor*. When an extra ballet was needed to make up the second triple bill for the revised programme, there was no time to make a new one, so a *divertissement* was got together under the title of *Le Festin*, mainly of pieces from ballets by Marius Petipa, including the *grand pas classique hongrois* from *Raymonda*, rightly regarded as one of his most brilliant classical compositions. Petipa, who is nowadays, thanks to *Swan Lake* and *The Sleeping Beauty*, the most widely known of all choreographers, was at that time unknown outside Russia; the Parisian journal *Le Théâtre* introduced him to its readers as 'the brother of the famous Petipa', meaning the French dancer and choreographer Lucien Petipa, who was the first Albrecht in *Giselle*.

Because of the reduced programme and the unexpected emphasis on ballet, at that time very lowly regarded in Paris, Diaghilev was no longer welcome at the Opéra. Instead, he booked the Châtelet Theatre, handsome but faded, which he recarpeted and partly redecorated for the occasion. Thus, more or less by accident, was born what became and remained for twenty years the most widely publicized ballet company in the world.

Valentin Serov: poster for Paris season, 1909
Anna Pavlova in *Les Sylphides*

THÉATRE DU CHÂTELET
SAISON RUSSE MAI JUIN 1909
OPÉRA ET BALLET

His company

The Diaghilev Ballet gave its first performance at the Châtelet Theatre, Paris, on 19 May 1909, with a *répétition générale* (or public final rehearsal) the night before. Even for the *répétition générale* evening dress was obligatory in every part of the theatre and patrons were warned that nobody would be admitted after the rise of the curtain at 8.30 precisely. Serge Grigoriev in his book about the company reproduces the programme of the *répétition générale*: one fascinating thing to be observed is that the name Diaghilev is nowhere visible on it. The title page says merely: 'Russian season with the participation of the artists, orchestra and choruses of the theatres of St Petersburg and Moscow.' The programme also makes it clear that the description (by Grigoriev and others) of how marvellously Chaliapin sang that night in *Prince Igor* must be based on a confused memory of another occasion, since he was not in that performance. But the dancers made an impressive list.

Pavlova and Fokine played the leads in *Le Pavillon d'Armide* (they were saved until the first night, Koralli and Mordkin dancing the rehearsal), but Nijinsky won even more admiration in his solo as a slave, dressed in old-fashioned style with a skirted jacket and plumed turban, his costume white and silver with a touch of yellow. Offstage, Nijinsky was, in Benois' words, 'more like a shop assistant than a fairy-tale hero'. Descriptions agree that he was short, rather thick-set, his neck enormous, his features somewhat Mongolian with a slightly sulky expression, and generally silent, with a habit of picking his fingers all the time. At rehearsal he performed with unfailing precision, but mechanically. But as he put on his costume, he seemed to change his placid nature into that of whatever being he saw reflected in his mirror. His appearance and manner as the elegant slave boy captivated the audience as much as the soaring height of his jumps astonished them.

Even Nijinsky's presence could not steal all the attention however: the character dancer George Rosay scored a great success as the leader of a jesters' dance in this ballet. Then in the dances in *Prince Igor* Adolf Bolm, a powerful man with tremendous vigour, swarthy and dominating, was the chief warrior and the slight, dark, bright-eyed Sophie Fedorova the principal Polovtsian girl. Finally, in *Le Festin* Tamara Karsavina danced the Bluebird *pas de deux* with Nijinsky, who appeared also in the dances from

Above: Le Pavillon d'Armide
Vaslav Nijinsky as Armida's favourite
slave
Anna Pavlova as Armida

Maxim Detoma:
portrait of Vaslav Nijinsky, about 1910

21

Raymonda. When a revised version of *Le Festin* was given the following year, the extract from *Raymonda* was omitted. Nijinsky then led the Lesginka, a stormy character dance, which was moved to end the *divertissement* instead of starting it.

Le Festin
Vaslav Nijinsky
in the Lesginka

Polovtsian dances from *Prince Igor*
(Michel Fokine)
Adolf Bolm as the chief warrior
Sophie Fedorova as a Polovtsian girl

Incidentally, Diaghilev's Paris season was not, as is often imagined, the first time dancers from the Russian Imperial Ballet had danced in western Europe. During the nineteenth century dancers had moved about fairly freely from one country to another and it was customary for stars to make guest appearances abroad. This tradition continued right up to Diaghilev's time: Bolm, for instance, had danced at the Empire Theatre in London in the summer of 1908, partnering the ballerina Lydia Kyasht, a classmate of Karsavina's. Immediately after Diaghilev's Paris season, too, on 28 June, eight of his dancers, headed by Karsavina, Baldina and Theodore Kosloff, opened a month's season at the London Coliseum, billed as 'The Russian Dancers—recently the rage of Paris'. Their dancing was greatly admired; the *Daily Mail*, for instance, wrote that 'it is the old classical school dancing which they illustrate, but raised to a pitch of dexterity and grace which has never been surpassed here in our generation, and never equalled except by Mme Genée ... All the women are of a fragile prettiness which makes instant appeal, while their figures are rounded and supple, showing no signs of the over-development of muscle so often noticeable in dancers of the severely trained ballet-skirt order.' Yet although the dancing aroused enthusiasm, it was nothing like the frenzy into which the full company had thrown Paris. This was mainly because of the superiority of Diaghilev's productions, with the large company in full ballets, but also partly because Diaghilev prepared the ground carefully to achieve the maximum effect.

The care taken in preparing and casting his programme was matched by the art with which it was presented to the Parisian public. Diaghilev had caused the theatre to be redecorated, had removed some seats to enlarge the orchestra, and had done away with the *strapontins*, folding seats at the ends of rows, on which French theatres customarily bundle extra spectators who must peer at the spectacle without any hope of dignity or comfort. Besides, when raising money for the season after his Russian backing fell through, he had somehow given the French impresario Gabriel Astruc the impression that it was Astruc's own idea to bring the ballet to Paris (the famous Diaghilev charm at work, no doubt), and Astruc, having obtained several backers, ensured a really gala occasion, even (according to report) filling the front row of the circle with pretty French actresses and dancers to give a festive appearance.

Les Sylphides (Michel Fokine)
Vaslav Nijinsky

Cleopatra (Michel Fokine)
Sophie Fedorova as Ta-hor

On the second programme of ballets, *Les Sylphides* (with Pavlova, Karsavina, the young Baldina and Nijinsky) was admired, but the audience really went wild over *Cleopatra* with its sultry passions and strong melodrama. Diaghilev had triumphed—to the extent that the company was invited to give some extra performances, including a special one of *Les Sylphides* before the President of the Republic and the diplomatic corps; and the season's last performance, on 19 June, was at the Opéra after all. Artistically and financially the season was a success, and a return the following year seemed almost inevitable.

Les Sylphides
Anna Pavlova

Les Sylphides
Tamara Karsavina

Giselle (Marius Petipa)
Vaslav Nijinsky as Albrecht

Again this was arranged, as in 1909, during the summer closure of the Imperial Theatres, so that the dancers could be free. This time they spent more than a month in Paris, dancing at the Opéra, preceded by a fortnight in Berlin, and with a couple of nights in Brussels thrown in. They performed only ballets this year, the previous year's repertory being supplemented with five more works. *Giselle* was one of these, and a revival of Fokine's *Carnaval* (created for a charity ball) another. Diaghilev devised another *divertissement*, this time under the title *Les Orientales*, and Fokine created two entirely new works, *The Firebird* and *Scheherazade*. Neither Pavlova nor Bolm was available, but the ballerina Ekaterina Geltzer and the leading male dancer Alexander Volinin from Moscow were invited, and in *Firebird* the young Lydia Lopokova, a dancer afterwards very much admired (especially in England) for her comic spirit, had her first leading role when Karsavina had to leave to fulfil another engagement (a London season with her supporting group). *Giselle*, even with Karsavina and Nijinsky, had a disappointing reception but *Carnaval*, *The Firebird* and *Scheherazade* were all liked.

Carnaval (Michel Fokine)
Tamara Karsavina: a portrait in her costume as Columbine

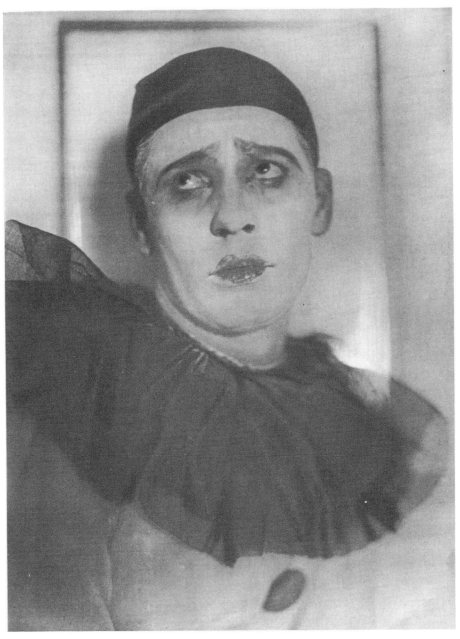

Carnaval
Adolf Bolm as Pierrot

Opposite: Carnaval
Fokine as Harlequin, Vera Fokina as Chiarina

The Firebird (Michel Fokine)
Left: Tamara Karsavina as the Firebird

Right: Alexei Bulgakov as the immortal Kostchei

The Firebird
Monsters in Kostchei's
kingdom

The Firebird
Adolf Bolm as Ivan
Tsarevitch, Tamara Karsavina
as the Firebird

Scheherazade (Michel Fokine)
Vaslav Nijinsky as the Golden Slave

It was the next year, 1911, which saw the Diaghilev Ballet established on a continuing basis. Diaghilev obtained engagements for a longer period, starting in Monte Carlo in the spring and continuing into the summer with their first visit to London after the usual Paris season. Some of the dancers he wanted (Karsavina, for instance) were senior enough to have contracts entitling them to take leave from the Imperial Theatres and were thus available outside the summer holiday period, and by pulling strings Diaghilev was able to get special permission for some others.

Nijinsky, however, being comparatively junior (he had graduated only in 1908 at the age of eighteen), would not have been free, but for an incident at a performance of *Giselle* in St Petersburg attended by the Dowager Empress and the Grand Duchess Xenia. Nijinsky had been given permission to wear the costumes designed by Benois for Diaghilev's production instead of the usual ones belonging to the theatre, but offence was taken because these did not include the trunks then customarily worn over tights. The details of this incident are disputed, but what is definite is that Nijinsky was dismissed. Some of Diaghilev's colleagues clearly thought he had engineered the whole business so that Nijinsky would be free; others claim that Diaghilev was taken by surprise and that, having failed to get Nijinsky reinstated, he then felt a responsibility to provide him with work in future and continued his company because of this. The view that it was deliberate seems more consistent with Diaghilev's nature and subsequent actions.

Nicholas Legat: caricature of Enrico Cecchetti, about 1890

Petrushka (Michel Fokine)
Tamara Karsavina and Vaslav Nijinsky in scene 2

Opposite: Le Spectre de la Rose (Michel Fokine)
Tamara Karsavina and Vaslav Nijinsky

At this time also Diaghilev engaged Enrico Cecchetti, an exceptionally talented Italian dancer and teacher who had worked for some time in Russia, to give daily lessons to his dancers—a necessary step both for the continued artistic development of his principals and to bring up to an acceptable standard the rather mixed collection he had found it necessary to engage for his *corps de ballet* (since the Petersburg and Moscow ensemble dancers were naturally not available during their own seasons). Fokine remained as chief choreographer, although he was no longer to dance because this distracted some attention from Nijinsky; and another key member of the group was Grigoriev as *régisseur*—a term which seems to have covered everything from company manager and stage director to responsibility (after Fokine's later departure) for rehearsing and maintaining the repertory.

There were four new works by Fokine that summer, including two of his greatest, *Petrushka* and *Le Spectre de la Rose*, in both of which Karsavina and Nijinsky scored further great successes, all the more admired because the ballets were so different in mood and style, one very 'Russian' and dramatic, the other softly romantic.

In Paris, Diaghilev confined the season to eight performances and concentrated mainly on the new works. For London, where he opened at Covent Garden on 21 June, he chose *Le Pavillon d'Armide*, *Carnaval* and *Prince Igor* to introduce the company, later adding *Le Spectre de la Rose*, *Les Sylphides*, *Scheherazade* and *Cleopatra*. On 26 June the company took part in a royal gala

Thamar (Michel Fokine)
Adolf Bolm as the Prince

to celebrate the coronation of King George V. Whereas Paris had been most impressed by the exotic, barbaric aspects of the repertory, it was the romantic works which had greatest success in London.

By now a more analytical response was possible than the initial surprise and wonder which the first Paris season had evoked. A very long article in *The Times* speculated on the difference between the art of the Russian ballet and that with which London was already familiar.

> That they dance better—the simplest explanation—is one of the most misleading, for the elusive differentia does not lie in technique. Certainly their technique is exquisite; all of them can do the most wonderful things with no appearance of effort, and they can do many sorts of wonderful

things ... The Russians, in fact, have so long since brought their technique of dancing, their command of their limbs and bodies, their instinct for balance, for energy without exertion, to the highest point, that they have been able to develop the art for which that technique exists—namely, the conveyance of choreographic ideas ... In Russia, the ballet has been essentially an aristocratic institution, maintained by an autocratic government for the use of the cultivated classes. It has not depended for its existence on giving immediate pleasure (the bane of all democratic arts), but has been able to follow its own bent. It has not had to husband the imaginative energies of the spectators, but, on the contrary, has been able to pursue the proper aim of all arts—to trouble and exert their imagination ... It is, in fact, not in the technical skill of the dancing, but in the variety and imaginative quality of those ideas which the dancing succeeds in expressing that the true differentia of the Russian ballet is to be found ... And above all there is restraint of emotion. For this is one of the first principles of the art of expressive dancing, that nothing must be taken too seriously ... It is immensely serious as Art, but never for a moment serious as Life.

So successful was Diaghilev's London season that he was invited to return to Covent Garden in the autumn. This time Karsavina was not available but he brought Pavlova—already known and popular in London from appearances with her own company—to dance *Giselle*, and Mathilde Kchessinskaya in *Swan Lake* (for which he bought the décor from the Bolshoi Theatre, Moscow). Diaghilev even took the trouble to engage the famous violinist Mischa Elman to play the solos for the two big duets, and a myth has grown up that he rushed to the theatre in a taxi between items during a concert he was giving at the Albert Hall. The story is such a good one that it is a pity there is not a word of truth in it. Oddly enough, Diaghilev's wish for Tchaikovsky's music to make its full effect did not prevent him from changing the score: Nijinsky danced his solo, for instance, to the music written for the Sugar Plum Fairy in *The Nutcracker*, and Kchessinskaya was permitted to insert one of her favourite solos to music by Kadletz.

Diaghilev planned to show his company that winter (1911–12) in St Petersburg and had engaged the best available theatre—the new but not very fashionable Narodny Dom (People's House). But it caught fire and was burned to the ground, and he had to find other engagements in Berlin, Vienna, Budapest and Paris at short notice. In fact his company and their works were never to be seen in his native land.

1912 was notable principally for the choreographic début of Nijinsky. Diaghilev had decided that he wanted a new choreographer with a new approach, and Nijinsky was receptive to his ideas; besides, it is now generally accepted that Diaghilev was in love with him. It appears that rehearsals of *L'Après-midi d'un Faune* had taken place secretly since the spring of 1911; the first performance was given on 29 May 1912 and the reception was very mixed. Nowadays the short scene of a faun's erotic imaginings and encounters with a group of nymphs looks innocuous enough and very beautiful, but at the time it caused a great scandal—and was the first time Diaghilev had experienced anything other than an enthusiastic or at least perfectly polite reception for one of his productions. Fokine's new works that year were also disappointingly received (although

Jeux (Vaslav Nijinsky)
Nijinsky

Opposite: Valentine Hugo:
drawing of Tamara
Karsavina, Vaslav
Nijinsky and Ludmilla
Schollar in *Jeux*, about
1913

Thamar, with its strong drama based on Georgian legend, survived many years) and, because of Diaghilev's growing interest in Nijinsky, Fokine decided to leave.

Astruc, Diaghilev's first Paris impresario, was responsible in 1913 for the opening season of the new Théâtre des Champs-Elysées and nearly bankrupted himself with the enormous sum he paid Diaghilev to participate in it with a mixed programme of operas (by singers specially assembled from Russia, headed of course by Chaliapin) and ballets. The main new ballet productions were by Nijinsky: Debussy's *Jeux*, treated as an angular encounter in a moonlit garden for a boy, two girls and a couple of tennis balls; and Stravinsky's *Rite of Spring*. The latter was a deliberately primitive evocation of prehistoric rites and ritual sacrifice. The dancers with their toes

turned in, their heads leaning sideways to be propped up by one arm, itself supported on the other fist, made an unusual sight, and their movements were strange and jerky too. The ballet was received at its first performance with shouts of derision and whistles, making it difficult for the dancers to hear the music. As they already had trouble in following the complex rhythms, this made them wonder how they would ever get through. They had another difficulty which can hardly have been apparent to the audience: Lydia Sokolova in her memoirs remarked that 'I do not know whether it was our wigs, or the smell of our hot flannel costumes, or the fact that there were so many of us packed together, or excitement, or fear, but we generated heat like a furnace; and at the end of the ballet there can have been none of the forty-odd dancers who was not soaking.'

Theodor Fedorovsky: costume design for *Khovanshchina*,
used as a programme cover for Paris season, 1913

Opposite: The Rite of Spring (Vaslav Nijinsky)
One of the *corps de ballet*

Later that year the company went on a South American tour during which Nijinsky suddenly married Romola de Pulszka, a Hungarian girl with money who had travelled with them as a prospective recruit. Shortly afterwards Nijinsky failed to perform one night, which according to Grigoriev necessitated teaching his role of Harlequin in *Carnaval* very hurriedly to another dancer, Alexander Gavrilov. When the tour was over Diaghilev (who had remained in Europe, having a superstitious dread of sea voyages) instructed Grigoriev to send a telegram stating that in view of his breach of contract Nijinsky's services were no longer required.

Because of this, Diaghilev persuaded Fokine to return as choreographer for the next season. The most successful of the works he staged was Rimsky-Korsakov's opera *Le Coq d'or*, presented with the singers at the side of the stage and all the action performed by dancers. (Years later Fokine was to revive this in a shortened all-ballet version.) *The Legend of Joseph*, to music by Richard Strauss, was also notable if only because it introduced, in the title role, a new dancer Diaghilev had seen and engaged in Moscow, Leonide Massine. The role of Potiphar's wife was played by an opera singer, Maria Kuznetsova—not the only time Diaghilev gave leading roles to a non-dancer; for instance, another singer, Flora Revalles, was later engaged to play leading parts in *Scheherazade* and *Cleopatra*.

The outbreak of war meant almost a year of inactivity for the company, but during 1915 Massine prepared his first ballet, *Soleil de Nuit*, which was presented in two charity matinées, in Geneva and Paris, at the end of December. On 1 January 1916 the re-formed company sailed for New York.

The principal dancers now were mostly new: Massine, the classic virtuoso Stanislas Idzikovsky, Gavrilov and the character dancer Leon Woizikovsky among the men; Lubov Tchernicheva, Lydia Sokolova and Vera Nemchinova among the women. Bolm and Lopokova were to join them in America—and also Nijinsky at the insistence of their American impresario. This entailed elaborate negotiations (including the intervention of the King of Spain) to get him out of internment in Austria–Hungary. He and Diaghilev did not get on at all well, and when the impresario, Otto Kahn, demanded Nijinsky's presence as a requisite for a further American tour later that year, the compromise was reached that Diaghilev would temporarily withdraw to Europe with Massine and a few dancers to prepare new ballets, and Nijinsky would take charge of the remaining company and sign the contract for the tour. The results were disastrous; Nijinsky announced a new ballet, *Til Eulenspiegel* (to Strauss' music) but did not finish it in time and the dancers had to improvise large sections during the dress rehearsal. In his everyday behaviour, too, Nijinsky was showing signs of the madness which soon overtook him; the season produced several embarrassments including some bad debts which apparently played a part in preventing the company from ever dancing in the United States again.

Meanwhile in Rome, where Diaghilev had made his temporary headquarters, his usual circle of friends (Bakst, Larionov, Gontcharova and Stravinsky) were joined by a couple of newcomers full of bright ideas, Picasso and Cocteau. Massine, having done a couple more small works, produced *The Good-Humoured Ladies*, a mannered and brittle comedy but

The Legend of Joseph (Michel Fokine)
Leonide Massine as Joseph

Leonide Massine, Natalia Gontcharova, Mikhail Larionov, Igor Stravinsky
and Leon Bakst at Lausanne, 1915

Opposite: Parade (Leonide Massine)
Leon Woizikovsky as the Manager in evening dress

brilliantly carried out, and the cubist circus fantasy *Parade* which was greatly
enjoyed by audiences and dancers and included such tricks as the choreographer, in his role as a Chinese conjurer, pretending to make an egg
disappear; not to mention a couple of cubist 'managers' and a pantomime
horse which sat down very elegantly.

During much of 1917 and 1918 the Diaghilev company was in Spain, the
only country where they could get suitable bookings during the war. Their
fortunes were very low; the dancers were at times on to reduced pay, or
even, for a while, none at all. The tours produced some remarkable inci-
dents, too, such as the time when they arrived in the town of Logroño to find
the management insisting on *Scheherazade* although the scenery and costumes were not available. The *Carnaval* curtains were used (at least they
were designed by Bakst!) and a ragbag of costumes from *Bluebird*, *Prince Igor*,
Cleopatra and other works. Sokolova describes Grigoriev, with an enormous

The Three-cornered Hat
(Leonide Massine)
Massine as the Miller

Opposite:
La Boutique Fantasque
Lydia Lopokova as the
Can-Can Dancer

old sword he had managed to borrow, stamping about at the end shouting: 'Die you fools! Die anywhere!' and adds: 'I forget whether I was struck down by the one and only sword, died by auto-suggestion, or got a friendly colleague to strangle me.' No doubt Grigoriev had this incident among others in mind when he recalled that 'our tour took us for the most part to smaller places in the Spanish provinces, where we met with many amusing adventures'.

After this and another South American tour (during which Nijinsky appeared with the company for the last time), they were glad to have a London engagement in 1918, even though it meant appearing as one turn on a variety bill at the Coliseum. This lasted for about six months; then in the spring of 1919 (after a brief visit to Manchester) they transferred to the Alhambra for a proper ballet season. This included the premières of two outstandingly successful works by Massine, *La Boutique Fantasque* with its story of dolls coming to life, and *The Three-cornered Hat*—an outcome of the time spent in Spain and the lessons in Spanish dancing Massine had from Felix Fernandez. With its Alarcón story, Falla music and Picasso designs, this is probably Massine's finest ballet. Karsavina rejoined for this season and Lopokova made her London début—but ran off without notice soon

La Boutique Fantasque
Mme Cecchetti as the Russian Wife, Stanislas Idzikovsky as the Snob

after the première of *Boutique*, so that Nemchinova had to take over her role of the can-can dancer. About this time Diaghilev began two distinctive practices: having a special front-curtain designed for almost every one of his ballets (he later sold some by Picasso to raise funds), and having musical interludes played to avoid long intervals which he thought displeased English audiences. Diaghilev always paid much attention to the musical side of his performances: he engaged first-rate conductors (Ansermet, Beecham, Boult, Desormière, Goossens and Monteux among them) and often included concert pieces in his programmes.

La Boutique Fantasque (Leonide Massine)
Massine as the Can-Can Dancer

The Sleeping Princess
(Marius Petipa)
Olga Spessivtseva as Princess
Aurora

Opposite: Daphnis and Chloe
(Michel Fokine)
Anton Dolin as Daphnis

During 1920, although there were no complaints about Massine's new ballets, he and Diaghilev began to quarrel, and early the next year Grigoriev was again instructed to depose the former favourite—this time in person, having to tell him at a rehearsal that he was no longer wanted and could leave at once. The first new productions of 1921 were therefore the first (and last) ballet of the dancer Tadeo Slavinsky, to music by Prokofiev, called *Chout* (a French transliteration of the Russian word for buffoon), and a group of Spanish dancers in their own self-contained *Cuadro Flamenco*, for which Diaghilev used a setting by Picasso.

The autumn of 1921 saw one of Diaghilev's most famous productions, however: *The Sleeping Princess* (his adaptation of *The Sleeping Beauty*). It is reported that he hoped to have a long run with this elaborate spectacle (music by Tchaikovsky, choreography by Petipa, designs by Bakst) and thus emulate the profits of the current hit show *Chu Chin Chow*; it also temporarily solved the problem of having no resident choreographer. But in spite of what was widely thought the excellence of the production, and in spite of strengthening the company with several dancers from Russia—Vera Trefilova, Lubov Egorova and Olga Spessivtseva, all former Petersburg dancers living in Paris, came to take turns as Princess Aurora; Pierre Vladimirov (who had already danced for Diaghilev before the war) came to play the Prince; and Carlotta Brianza, the original Aurora, was brought over to play the wicked fairy Carabosse—the ballet was immensely admired but failed to draw the crowds; it had to be taken off long before Diaghilev could repay his backer, Sir Oswald Stoll. There were, in consequence, only modest new productions the next year (1922): the last act of *The Sleeping Princess* with an improvised setting and costumes (since Oswald Stoll had kept the Bakst designs), and Stravinsky's simple, four-character fable *Renard* produced by Bronislava Nijinska, who had already done some extra choreography for *The Sleeping Princess*. The next year, however, Nijinska produced her masterpiece, *Les Noces*, a stern setting of a Russian peasant wedding in abstract terms, and the year after that the gaily mocking *Les Biches*.

Enrico Cecchetti and Serge Lifar, 1924

New dancers became prominent: Anton Dolin and Serge Lifar were both given careful grooming, Alice Nikitina and Alexandra Danilova began to dance leading roles, and later the very young Alicia Markova began to be prepared for big things.

Romeo and Juliet (Bronislava Nijinska)
Serge Lifar and Alice Nikitina

Le Chant du Rossignol (George Balanchine)
Alicia Markova as the Nightingale

Les Matelots (Leonide Massine)
Rehearsal with Tadeo Slavinsky, Vera Nemchinova, Leon Woizikovsky, Lydia Sokolova, Serge Lifar

After another year with Nijinska as choreographer, Massine was brought back for a time, then a new young man was tried out, George Balanchine, who had recently arrived from Russia as a dancer. He and Massine both did several works in the final seasons, notably *Les Matelots* (a bright comedy) and the enigmatic *Ode* by Massine, and Balanchine's *Apollo* and *The Prodigal Son*. *Apollo* has been widely accepted as one of the finest of all twentieth-century ballets. Lifar also was allowed to try his first ballet, a new version of *Renard*.

During 1928 Diaghilev became a little worried by possible competition from a new company formed in Paris by Ida Rubinstein, a rich amateur who (as a pupil of Fokine) had in the early seasons of his company taken roles where looks and acting mattered more than dancing. Hitherto, competition had not appeared to concern him. Pavlova had her own company which toured extensively, there were innumerable splinter groups of his own dancers who went off to tour independently, and from 1920 to 1925 there was in fact a company, Les Ballets Suédois, which provided a serious artistic challenge to Diaghilev with many distinguished creations involving composers like Auric, Honneger, Milhaud, Poulenc, Satie and Cole Porter, and designers including de Chirico and Léger. Yet none of these appears to have caused alarm. Perhaps Rubinstein's company was taken seriously as a threat because some of Diaghilev's own collaborators were taking part, among them Massine, Nijinska and Stravinsky. Or perhaps Diaghilev had lost some of his old resilience.

Ode (Leonide Massine)

Certainly he was showing less active interest in his company. His health had deteriorated, his emotional life seems not to have been happy and he became increasingly obsessed with his collection of rare books. He was less likely to attend rehearsals, leaving others to supervise the works in progress. He astonished Grigoriev in 1928 by saying he did not much care whether or not Balanchine's contract was renewed. At the end of the summer season at Covent Garden in 1929 he went off to Paris after assembling the company on stage to wish them good holidays and tell them that for the first time ever he had an uninterrupted series of engagements for the following year already signed. The company gave a week in Vichy and then dispersed after a final performance on 4 August. On 19 August, holidaying at Monte Carlo, Grigoriev received a telegram: 'Diaghilev died this morning. Inform company. Lifar.' He was buried where he died, in Venice.

It would be hard to explain exactly Diaghilev's part in the company's work. He raised funds, secured illustrious patrons, brought people together, gave them ideas, commented on the way they tried to work and arranged the lighting of the ballets. He told his dancers how to make up for the stage, how to deport themselves off stage; if he thought they had promise he told them what to see and what to think. Maybe he was really just a catalyst. After his death there was a half-hearted attempt to continue the company. But nobody really had the spirit left to go on, and everyone drifted away.

And ballet afterwards was never the same as it had been before Diaghilev.

His choreographers

With his art exhibitions and his seasons of concerts and operas, Diaghilev's aim had been to introduce the west to what he regarded as the best of Russian art: not just a haphazard collection but a careful selection—with, in the case of the paintings, quite a lot of new works by his friends and collaborators. Similarly, what was called under his direction the Russian Ballet was rather different from anything to be seen in Russia at that or any other time.

It is true that he presented a certain number of traditional works—and it is odd to think that when in 1921 he produced *The Sleeping Beauty* (renamed *The Sleeping Princess* for the occasion) this was thought a very old-fashioned ballet, needing some amendment of its music and choreography before it could be acceptable, and an elaborate explanatory introduction in the programme. This was in spite of the fact that the ballet, the joint masterpiece of Petipa and Tchaikovsky, was at that time markedly younger than even the latest of Diaghilev's own surviving ballets are today. Maybe Diaghilev was remembering what happened with *Le Festin* on his very first programme. This introduced highlights from several of Petipa's ballets, including Karsavina and Nijinsky in the virtuoso Bluebird *pas de deux* from *The Sleeping Beauty* (called on the programme, for some reason, *The Firebird*—this duet had several different titles in Diaghilev's repertory from time to time, including *La Princesse enchantée* and *L'Oiseau d'or*). Nijinsky also danced in another of the Petipa fragments in *Le Festin*, the *grand pas classique* from *Raymonda* with its famous male *pas de quatre*, but in spite of this Petipa's works caused far less of a stir than the new works on the programme.

During his early seasons, however, Diaghilev continued to mount old ballets like *Giselle* and a shortened version of *Swan Lake*, besides occasionally inviting established choreographers from Russia: Boris Romanov, whose two productions for Diaghilev caused no great stir, and Alexander Gorsky, who might have proved far more interesting but was prevented from coming because Tcherepnin did not finish in time the music for their intended ballet *The Red Masks*.

Valentin Serov: portrait of
Michel Fokine, about 1907

The main burden of the repertory for the company's first six years, however, except for the season when Nijinsky was made principal choreographer, fell on Michel Fokine. Between 1909 and 1914 he revived four of his existing ballets in revised versions and created fourteen new ones, besides contributing to *Le Festin* and producing *Giselle* with at least one additional passage of dancing, the fugue for the wilis which had previously been omitted and forgotten. This is an impressive output, especially when you remember that some of the new works were made to music which the dancers and presumably the choreographer also found advanced in manner and rhythmically difficult to follow. Seven of Fokine's ballets from this period are still being danced today and almost all of these are among the few ballets which are known by name to the general public. They fall into two distinct styles: the powerfully exotic (*Scheherazade, The Firebird, Petrushka* and the dances from *Prince Igor*) and the lyrically romantic (*Les Sylphides,*

61

Carnaval, Le Spectre de la Rose). Compared with the best works of Diaghilev's later choreographers, Fokine's ballets are rather simple and straightforward; partly because of this they have always made an immediate appeal to the public and, when carefully mounted, show no sign of losing that appeal.

The fact that Fokine had begun to make his name before Diaghilev formed his company (his growing reputation was in fact one of the arguments Benois used for starting the venture) should disprove the suggestion sometimes made that all Diaghilev's choreographers owed everything to his guidance. Fokine went on working long after he left Diaghilev, and it must be granted that few of his later works were as good as these early ballets; but he did manage to regain his old form sometimes, and after such a tremendous spurt of effort it should not be surprising if his inspiration was played out for a while. All the same, it is clear that Fokine in his prime benefited from the close association with artists like Benois and Bakst and a composer like Stravinsky which he enjoyed in his Diaghilev days. It is equally clear that without his presence there would probably never have been a Diaghilev Ballet at all, and that the success of the Paris seasons almost certainly owed more to Fokine's contributions than to those of any other individual. So the benefit was fairly shared on both sides.

The experiment of appointing Nijinsky as chief choreographer seems to have been generally regarded at the time as disastrous. Diaghilev's motive was to find a talent responsive to new ideas, and one which he could mould according to his own theories, which at that time included an inordinately high regard for the music-visualization theories of Dalcroze and his method of eurhythmics. Curiously, there seems little evidence of the effect of these theories in Nijinsky's one surviving work, *L'Après-midi d'un Faune*; and curiously also, that work shows an exceptionally strong plastic and atmos-

Les Sylphides (Michel Fokine)

L'Après-midi d'un Faune (Vaslav Nijinsky)
left: Nijinsky as the Faun; *right:* Bronislava Nijinska as a Nymph

pheric sense, suggesting that maybe Nijinsky was a rather better choreographer than he gets credit for. Massine in his autobiography expressed
great admiration for the meticulous way Nijinsky explained each small detail
when rehearsing *Faune* and said categorically that in different circumstances
Nijinsky would have been a great choreographer. His *Sacre du Printemps*
also, although difficult and unappreciated, was thought by some to have a
quality of pathos which Massine's later, better-organized version lacked.

Diaghilev seems to have cherished a strong wish to influence choreography. He was credited as the 'arranger' of *Les Orientales* (a *divertissement*
including Nijinsky's first choreography—a solo for himself) and he also
produced *Fireworks*, in which a complicated pattern of lights was played
through some plastic cubist scenery during a performance of music by
Stravinsky—nowadays we would call it a mixed-media event. But he real-
ized that, without any training as a dancer, he could not himself create
dances, and so had to achieve his ambition by influencing others.

Pablo Picasso: portrait of
Leonide Massine, 1917

Mikhail Larionov: drawing of Leonide Massine and Serge Diaghilev at rehearsal, about 1919
By courtesy of Sotheby & Co.

Kikimora (Leonide Massine)
Maria Shabelska as Kikimora

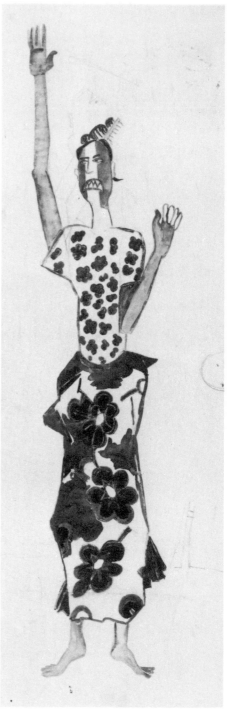

Mikhail Larionov: costume design for
Kikimora, 1916

66

However, his next protégé after Nijinsky proved rather stubborn. Massine's first efforts were put under the guidance of Larionov—short ballets in Russian folklore style, deliberately modelled after Fokine's manner. 'Of course he's rather provincial,' said Diaghilev, 'but we'll soon put an end to that.' Once the pupil had shown promise, Diaghilev himself began attending rehearsals, criticizing and making suggestions. He also encouraged Massine to buy a collection of old books of choreographic theory and example (by Blasis, Feuillet and others) which served to give his ideas a strong intellectual basis. Yet the dry, jerky mannered style which Massine evolved (slightly reminiscent of old silent films) seems so different from anything done by any of Diaghilev's other choreographers that it must contain much that is personal to Massine himself. And when Cocteau and Picasso came up with novel ideas for producing *Parade* to incorporate elements of circus and music-hall, plus a cubist stylization, Massine accepted their ideas readily and with understanding. Besides, Massine proved stubbornly resistant to some of Diaghilev's ideas: he insisted on his own way, against Diaghilev's wishes, in the treatment of the dances in *Le Astuzie Femminili*, for instance, and during one of his later periods with the company reworked his first ballet *Soleil de Nuit*, possibly feeling that he had been too much influenced by his mentors. (Diaghilev was furious and insisted on the old version being given instead.) Massine also produced at least one of his best ballets (*Le Beau Danube*) during his absences from Diaghilev's company, and after Diaghilev's death went on to devise completely new theories of creating ballets to symphonic music, becoming for many years the most highly regarded choreographer of his day.

Diaghilev's main achievement with Massine, in fact, was merely in persuading him to stay in ballet (he had thought of turning to acting); once Diaghilev had done this and given Massine's ambition the first impetus, the young man proved as strong-willed and independent as his master. Yet Diaghilev was crucially instrumental in deciding the details of two of Massine's most popular ballets: *La Boutique Fantasque* with its theme of dolls coming to life, and *The Three-cornered Hat* in which Massine uniquely succeeded in bringing the spirit of Spain into ballet. On the other hand, it was Massine's own gift of comic characterization which made the most lasting of his contributions to the art.

After trying out the young dancer Tadeo Slavinsky as choreographer, without success, Diaghilev turned next to Nijinsky's sister Bronislava Nijinska, who had already produced some ballets in Russia and appears in consequence to have been given a rather more free hand. Her creations for Diaghilev included two of the best works his company produced, *Les Noces* and *Les Biches*, the one as frivolously gay (although with undertones of rather wicked social comment) as the other was stern and austere. What they had in common was a personal use of movement which, on revival forty years later, proved completely unharmed by subsequent changes in fashion. Nijinska never produced anything else as good as these two ballets, but she had great skill in showing off dancers to good advantage and continued a successful career after leaving Diaghilev.

George Balanchine, the last of Diaghilev's important choreographers, had

Natalia Gontcharova:
design for scene 4, *Les
Noces*, 1923

Le Train Bleu (Bronislava
Nijinska)

Les Biches (Bronislava Nijinska)
Vera Nemchinova and Anatole Vilzak in the *andantino*

also begun his career in Russia before joining Diaghilev, and his accounts of experimental work by himself and the older Goleizovsky influenced Diaghilev in trying him out. He also quickly proved proficient and was willing to accept Diaghilev's suggestions. The beginning of his maturity as a choreographer, however, came with his first close working with Stravinsky on *Apollo*; the simplicity with which Stravinsky achieved his effects in this score led Balanchine to strip down the elaborations of his own youthful exuberance and develop the pure classicism on which his later fame was based. As a personal choice, if only one of Diaghilev's ballets could be saved for the future, I would choose *Apollo*, for its pure beauty and its expressive use of the classic style.

Apollo (George Balanchine)
Alice Nikitina as Terpsichore, Serge Lifar as Apollo

Apollo
Final tableau

The Prodigal Son (George Balanchine)
Serge Lifar as the Prodigal, Anton Dolin and Leon Woizikovsky as his Friends

72

By then, Diaghilev's career was nearly over. Balanchine consolidated his reputation with three more works in a short time (including his extraordinarily moving *Prodigal Son*) and then Diaghilev died. It took Balanchine longer than it had taken Massine to win fame without Diaghilev's assistance, but once he did so it proved longer lasting. Now, as director of New York City Ballet (which, under his guidance, has become in a few years one of the most highly regarded companies in the world) and as a choreographer for other companies, he has achieved an unmatched position with his ballets performed more widely and more often than has ever been the case with any other living choreographer.

The Prodigal Son
Serge Lifar as the Prodigal, Michael Fedorov as the Father

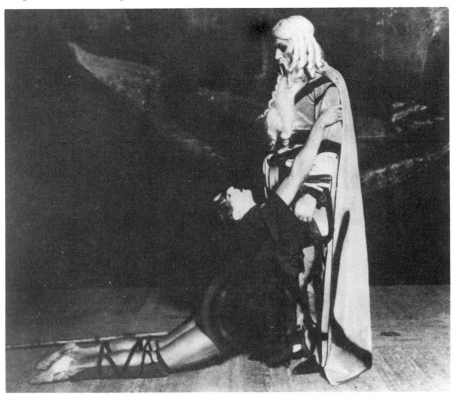

Le Renard (Serge Lifar)
Rehearsal

In his last season, Diaghilev tried out one more choreographic newcomer: Serge Lifar. His new version of Stravinsky's *Renard* achieved some notoriety by the ingenious idea of having a double cast of dancers and acrobats, identically dressed and masked, so that the audience would think the same person was doing an amazing range of actions. Later, Lifar established himself for many years as the outstanding influence on French ballet, although he was never greatly admired in Britain or America.

For all his constant seeking after novelty, two things must be said very firmly in favour of Diaghilev's policy in regard to choreography, namely that he was consistent in seeking to extend the scope of the art, and skilled in spotting new talent that deserved opportunity. Few companies if any have been so consistently successful in achieving at least a certain measure of success with one new choreographer after another. Few have taken such care to guide their newcomers and give them apt collaborators, but equally there must have been in Diaghilev's make-up a large measure of sheer flair for discovering ability.

He himself put his policy very simply: 'What's wanted [he told Grigoriev] is something quite different: a movement of liberation in choreography; some fresh form of achievement.'

Alexander Benois: design for Armida's costume in *Le Pavillon d'Armide*, 1907

His designers

'It was no accident,' wrote Benois, 'that what was afterwards known as the Ballets Russes was originally conceived not by the professionals of the dance but by a circle of artists, linked together by the idea of Art as an entity. Everything followed from the common desire of several painters and musicians to see the fulfilment of the theatrical dreams which haunted them.'

Until Diaghilev arrived Benois was without question the leader of this circle, and even later he was given for a while the title of artistic director to Diaghilev's company. In his theatrical aims, Benois admitted three important influences. First, the dancer Virginia Zucchi, who by the expressiveness of her dancing convinced him as a young man that ballet could be a serious art. Secondly, the painters Korovin and Golovin who both took part as designers in the theatrical seasons of Sava Mamontov's private opera company in Moscow and showed that décors could have high artistic value. Thirdly, the immense success of the Meiningen theatrical company which visited Petersburg in 1885 and 1890 and of their producer Chronegk in achieving a co-ordinated ensemble. In fact Benois said his ambition was to be a second Chronegk—'I wanted to become a stage painter only in order to be able "to do everything in the theatre", to be complete master and manager of the stage.'

Le Pavillon d'Armide, the first ballet danced by Diaghilev's company, was conceived entirely by Benois in an attempt to recreate the manners and appearance of the eighteenth century. His original idea of a three-act ballet was cut down to one because one-act ballets were growing more popular by the time the work was first produced by the Imperial Theatre in 1907 (so much for the myth that Diaghilev invented or popularized short ballets) but Benois agreed this was an improvement. It resulted in an unusual structure: a long dream *divertissement* for the middle scene, with short scenes, all mime and no dancing, to begin and end. Benois wanted it to be serious but at the same time sparkling and sumptuous, and it seems he achieved this. But we would not regard it today, I imagine, as at all a modern ballet, rather an adaptation of the tradition in which Petipa had worked during the nineteenth century, with a solid plot and set dances. (Benois actually told Fokine to take scenes from *The Sleeping Beauty* as his model.)

Alexander Benois: design for dream scene with *pas de trois* in *Le Pavillon d'Armide*

Alexander Benois: design from Petrushka's costume, *Petrushka*, 1911

Benois' great lasting contribution to ballet, and a far more original work, came in the company's third season: *Petrushka*. Benois had already left the company (Diaghilev had a curious predilection for setting him and Bakst at loggerheads) but was persuaded to return—Diaghilev travelled specially to Lugano from Petersburg for the purpose—because he was so suitable for helping realize the new ballet Stravinsky was already writing. The general

Alexander Benois: design for the Ballerina's costume, *Petrushka*

subject, that of the traditional puppet Petrushka, was already settled, but Benois invented many of the details, including the fundamental idea of a stage within the stage. He also designed the settings and costumes which are one of the most famous incarnations of an aspect of traditional Russian life, the spring fairs which had in fact by 1911 already been stamped out to prevent drunkenness and disorder.

79

Alexander Benois: design for a Street Dancer's costume, *Petrushka*

Petrushka
Bronislava Nijinska as the Street Dancer

Alexander Benois: design for act 1, *Giselle*, 1910

The other notable designs by Benois were for two romantic ballets where his feeling for atmosphere was valuable: *Les Sylphides* in 1909 and *Giselle* a year later. His also was the idea of staging the opera *The Golden Cockerel* with the singers massed at the sides of the stage and the action performed by dancers (1914). That same year he designed one more opera for Diaghilev, Stravinsky's *Le Rossignol*, and that was almost his last connexion with the company he had done so much to inspire. When he returned briefly in 1924 to design two Gounod operas, *Le Médecin Malgré Lui* and *Philémon and Baucis*, he complained that 'Diaghilev no longer likes my décors. I can't understand it.'

It is a curious thing that, with the solitary exception of Bakst, all the designers who had worked for the first five seasons of the Diaghilev Ballet were dropped after the sixth. Partly this could be explained by the outbreak of war, cutting Diaghilev off from his Russian contacts, but partly it reflected a change of taste. The early designers were Russian painters like Roerich (who did the brooding scene for the Polovtsian dances from *Prince Igor*, and also *The Rite of Spring*), and Golovin, whose designs for the first version of *Firebird* were a shimmering web of magic. Anisfeldt, Doboujinsky, Korovin and Soudeikin, all Russians, also contributed during this period when exoticism was the quality most admired and sought in the Russian performances.

Nikolai Roerich: design for *Prince Igor*, 1909

But the man who achieved most in the way of exoticism, and also proved versatile enough to remain influential even later, was Leon Bakst. His *Cleopatra* in the first season was delicately coloured: a temple of rose and gold, with a strip of green Nile seen between the columns. *Carnaval* the next year was also delicate with its Biedermeyer figures set against purplish blue curtains relieved only by two striped sofas and a high frieze. But with *Scheherazade*, also in 1910, Bakst really set the town on fire. Even nowadays, performances of this ballet are interrupted by a burst of applause as the curtain rises on that setting of rich reds and blues and greens, furnished with huge carpets, draped with lavish curtains, hung with golden lamps, piled voluptuously with huge cushions and filled by the sedulously attentive women of the sultan's court. Who else before Bakst had dared to mingle such oranges and crimsons, to offer such a luxurious swirl of ornament, to hint at such wickedness—although without actually going beyond the bounds of propriety? (His costume designs frequently show the women's breasts or bottoms exposed, but the versions worn on stage were more cautious.)

One result of *Scheherazade* was that within a few months women in Paris and London were going about in clothes which looked vaguely oriental. Their figures were no longer heavily corseted into an S-shape, their waists were freer but their skirts narrower: a few went so far as to wear 'harem skirts' but most compromised with the hobble skirt. Colours changed too, becoming bright, with more decoration. And a very similar change came over tastes in home furnishing: bright cushions everywhere, and ornate lamps which were sometimes even modelled into designs based on figures from Bakst's ballet. Orientalism in clothes has already been introduced into high fashion in Paris by the dressmaker Paul Poiret, but it was the Russian ballet in general and Bakst in particular who caused a new wave of taste to sweep through society.

Pablo Picasso: portrait of Leon Bakst, 1922

Informal dress for 1911, designed by Paul Poiret, drawn by Georges Lepape

Opposite: Day dress for 1908, drawn by 'Lucy'

Leon Bakst: *Modern dress*, 1910
By courtesy of Sotheby & Co.

Opposite: Leon Bakst: costume for the Marquis di Luca, *The Good-Humoured Ladies*, 1917

Leon Bakst: costume for Chloe, *Daphnis and Chloe*, 1912

Opposite: Leon Bakst: costume for a Boetian, *Narcisse*, 1911

Bakst's exotic side was seen again in ballets like *Thamar* (Georgian), *L'Après-midi d'un Faune* (a stylized ancient Greece) and *Daphnis and Chloe* (Greece again), but he also continued to develop his more delicate mood as in *Le Spectre de la Rose* and *Jeux*, set respectively in a girl's chaste bedroom and a nocturnal garden. Bakst was to return later, after all the other early designers had left, for *The Good-Humoured Ladies* in 1917 and the grandly elaborate production of *The Sleeping Princess* in 1921 which, for imaginative spectacle and evocation of past glories, remains unmatched.

Leon Bakst: costume for the Mountain Ash Fairy, *The Sleeping Princess*, 1921

Fée Canari

Mme Egorova

Tutu'
attachez au manteau
les manches!
on dansera san manches
otant le manteau

Bakst 192

Leon Bakst: costume for the Canary Fairy, *The Sleeping Princess*
By courtesy of Sotheby & Co.

Natalia Gontcharova:
costume for Prince Guidon,
Le Coq d'or, 1914

By then, however, Diaghilev had tried many other modes. A couple of painters brought from Russia in 1914, Natalia Gontcharova and Mikhail Larionov (inventors of 'cubist rayonism') had an immense influence. In Moscow they and their followers had attracted attention by wearing green or purple wigs and bright clothes, and painting flowers, birds or even elephants on their faces. Gontcharova in *Le Coq d'or* and Larionov in *Soleil de Nuit* and *Contes Russes* showed a new aspect of Russian folk tradition: bright and simple like a children's tale. Their designs were fun (although not always fun to dance in, since the costumes were often heavy and padded).

Natalia Gontcharova: sketches for costume designs, *Les Noces*, 1923
(also opposite)

N. Gontchova

These two remained with Diaghilev for many years. Gontcharova produced some of the company's most enduring designs, still used and admired today, for the plain settings of Nijinska's *Les Noces* and the bright new version of *Firebird* created after the old scenery had been ruined. Larionov was set—a surprising job for a painter, and explicable only in the light of the early influence of painters in Diaghilev's company—to supervise in turn the early efforts of three aspirant choreographers: Massine, Slavinsky and Lifar. Larionov also produced a large number of caricatures which reveal a great deal about the daily life of the company.

Pablo Picasso: sketch for scenery, *The Three-cornered Hat*, 1919

Opposite: Pablo Picasso and Leonide Massine at Pompeii, 1917

The next important acquisition was Picasso. He made his first designs for Diaghilev in 1917—the cubist *Parade*, followed by several other works of which the most important were *The Three-cornered Hat* and *Pulcinella*. If we exclude Sert (whose designs for *The Legend of Joseph* had proved far too heavy) and the American Robert E. Jones, brought in for Nijinsky's ill-fated *Til Eulenspiegel*, Picasso was the first of the western artists who worked for Diaghilev all through his second decade. Their names are like a rollcall of the artists, major and minor, of the time: Derain, Matisse, Juan Gris, Marie Laurençin, Braque, Henri Laurens, Chanel, Pedro Pruna, Utrillo, Ernst and Miró, Gabo and Pevsner, Yakulov, Tchelichev, Bouchant, de Chirico, Rouault. But very few of them designed more than one ballet, and none of

Pablo Picasso: costume for the Jota, *The Three-cornered Hat*

André Derain: costume for an English lady, *La Boutique Fantasque*, 1919

Pablo Picasso: costume for Pimpinella, *Pulcinella*, 1920
Opposite: Tamara Karsavina as Pimpinella, *Pulcinella*

104

Henri Matisse: sketch for front curtain, *Le Chant du Rossignol*, 1920

Opposite:
Henri Matisse, Leonide Massine and the Nightingale at rehearsal, 1920

them more than two. During the 1920s Diaghilev tried one style after another: constructivism, cubism, surrealism, social realism and others. Many new movements in turn were reflected in his repertory, and each was brought to a wide public much more quickly than would otherwise have been the case. But it is difficult to see that Diaghilev was still making fashion as he had done in his early days when he and his colleagues planned their work on a long-term continuing basis. Some of his designs were very fine, others were rather silly. But they were no longer setting the trends, they were following them, however smartly and wittily.

Marie Laurençin: sketch for *Les Biches*, 1924

Georges Braque: costume for Muse,
Zephire et Flore, 1925

Pedro Pruna: design for curtain, *Les Matelots*,
1925

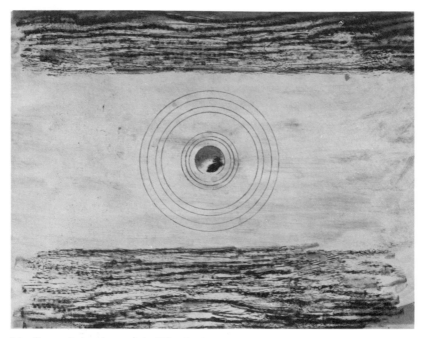

Max Ernst: design for curtain ('The Sea'), *Romeo and Juliet*, 1926

Naum Gabo and Anton Pevsner: constructions for *La Chatte*, 1927

Pavel Tchelichev: designs for *Ode*, 1928
(also below)

Giorgio de Chirico: Alexandra Danilova and Anton Dolin in scene 2, *Le Bal*, 1929

Giorgio de Chirico: design for scene 2, *Le Bal*

Georges Rouault: design for scene 1, *The Prodigal Son*, 1929

His composers

When Diaghilev gave up his aspirations to be a composer, he clearly gave them up for good; there is no suggestion in any of the accounts of his company that he was ever tempted even to undertake the arrangement of anyone else's music himself. His knowledge of music clearly remained useful to him, all the same. Grigoriev describes how he was able to play a piano version of the revised score of *Cleopatra* to his colleagues, explaining to Fokine exactly what alterations had been made: 'He played very well, biting his tongue the whole time, especially when he came to the difficult bits.'

He was also prepared to go to immense trouble over the music for his ballets. When he had decided, for instance, that Massine was to create *The Good-Humoured Ladies* on the plot of Goldoni's play, it was Diaghilev who suggested Scarlatti as the most suitable composer and, with Massine, he went through about five hundred of Scarlatti's sonatas to choose the twenty or so which would best serve their purpose.

He had no hesitation in commenting on the work of those composers who wrote music specially for him. Hence the note which Vittorio Rieti sent him with the final version of *Le Bal* after many alterations at Diaghilev's request, saying: 'Here is *Le Bal*. It is dedicated to you; it is for you; do whatever you like with it, but above all do not hope that I will do any more to it.'

In his first season Diaghilev used only existing music, and the following year also, with one exception. The exception, however, was rather an important one, because the first score composed expressly to Diaghilev's commission was *The Firebird*. Stravinsky was about twenty-seven when it was commissioned, and regarded at best as a promising newcomer. Diaghilev had been impressed by his *Fireworks* which he heard at a concert (and which he later presented in a semi-staged version, see page 64) and insisted on letting him write *Firebird* despite a marked lack of enthusiasm on the part of all the others in his unofficial committee. Diaghilev admired Stravinsky's music precisely for the qualities of novelty and originality

Igor Stravinsky, about 1914

which put off his friends; they found its rhythms too difficult for dancing which seems as absurd now as the similar complaint an earlier generation had made against Tchaikovsky. Now that Stravinsky is securely established as the greatest ballet composer of his time, it is difficult to imagine how revolutionary his early music once sounded—but perhaps one can guess the effect they must once have had by analogy with the strangeness of some of Stravinsky's recent scores at first hearing, until one has assimilated their novelty.

But if *Firebird* and *Petrushka* were thought difficult, *The Rite of Spring* caused a riot—literally, with people hitting each other during the première. After that, his opera *Le Rossignol* must have seemed almost tame. The reception of *Rite* put Stravinsky off writing ballets for some time, but later Diaghilev commissioned *Pulcinella* and *Les Noces* from him, besides presenting the ballets *Le Chant du Rossignol* (adapted by Stravinsky from the opera), *Renard* and *Apollo*, and the operas *Mavra* and *Oedipus Rex*.

It might be that Stravinsky would have been drawn to ballet anyway, but it was Diaghilev who first discovered his aptitude for it.

Stravinsky, like most of the other composers in the early seasons, was Russian; the success of those early years was mainly in the more nationalistic works. But from the fourth season onwards foreign composers (mainly French) began to be introduced into the programmes. Do not imagine that the actual repertory of the Diaghilev Ballet was always on a distinguished level; among the composers who wrote specially for the company were several whose names are somewhat less than household words.

Diaghilev seems in fact to have had a mixed attitude to music: capable on the one hand of discovering Stravinsky, on the other of suggesting the horrifying hotchpotch by different composers in different styles which was adopted for *Cleopatra*. He also foreshadowed later experiments in ballets without music when he made Massine try out a piece called *Liturgie* (abandoned without ever being publicly shown) in which the only accompaniment was to be rhythmical stamping.

He defended his use of foreign composers—and designers too—by asking: 'How can we find young Russian musicians and painters abroad?' But he was not cut off from his homeland until war broke out in 1914, followed by revolution three years later. By 1914 he had already used music by half a dozen French and German composers, including commissioned scores by Ravel (*Daphnis and Chloe*), Debussy (*Jeux*) and Richard Strauss (*The Legend of Joseph*).

Pablo Picasso: portrait of Igor Stravinsky, 1917

115

Vaslav Nijinsky and Maurice Ravel, 1912

Opposite: Pablo Picasso: portrait of Manuel de Falla, 1920

9-6-20

Jean Oberlé: caricature of Georges Auric, Darius Milhaud, Francis Poulenc, Jean Cocteau and Erik Satie, about 1917

Opposite: Pablo Picasso: portrait of Erik Satie, 1920

Under the influence of Cocteau, Diaghilev turned to Satie for *Parade* (and later used music by this once under-regarded composer for two light-hearted ballets); also from 1924 onwards he had a set of mainly frivolous works specially written by the young wave of French composers: Poulenc (*Les Biches* is perhaps the best thing he ever wrote), Auric, Milhaud and Sauguet. He also, perhaps because London like Paris was one of his most regular ports of call, mounted a small group of ballets with English music. Constant Lambert's *Romeo and Juliet*, although not liked at the time, introduced a young man who was later going to play a vital part in founding British ballet (it was commissioned after the twenty-year-old boy sent Diaghilev a *suite de danses* complete with scenario which Diaghilev rejected but the Camargo Society later used). Lord Berners, who wrote *The Triumph of Neptune*, was also later associated with the Sadlers Wells Ballet, and that company's repertory included a new version of *The Gods Go A'Begging* which Diaghilev first presented to a score arranged by Thomas Beecham from music by Handel.

14-5-20-

119

Yet these and other composers during the 1920s were mostly used once only. Exceptions were Auric (who wrote *Les Facheux, Les Matelots* and *Pastorale*) and Rieti (*Barabau* and *Le Bal*). Apart from these, the only recurring names among the composers are the two Russians Stravinsky and Prokofiev.

Prokofiev's position was rather different from that of Stravinsky who had settled permanently in the west. Prokofiev remained a Soviet citizen and returned to Russia to become the most important composer of Soviet ballet. His first two works for Diaghilev also kept a strong Russian flavour. *Chout* was a modern treatment of a Russian fairy story. *Le Pas d'Acier* was supposed

Opposite: Natalia Gontcharova: portrait of Serge Prokofiev, 1921

The Triumph of Neptune (Lord Berners)
Lord Berners with Serge Lifar and Alexandra Danilova

Mikhail Larionov: caricature of himself, Serge Prokofiev and Serge Diaghilev at a rehearsal of *Chout*, 1921
By courtesy of Sotheby & Co.

122

Le Pas d'Acier (Serge Prokofiev)
Lubov Tchernicheva, Serge Lifar

to treat themes from contemporary Russian life, that of peasants in one
scene and factory workers in the other—although most people found some
difficulty in following it. But Prokofiev's third ballet for Diaghilev (the last
his company was to produce) was *The Prodigal Son* which, in spite of its
biblical derivation, was a fairly universal theme of strong emotional appeal
that was matched by the music as well as the other elements (choreography,
design and performance) of its production. So in respect of new music
Diaghilev ended his ballet career as he had begun it, by being responsible for
the writing of a fine score by one of his countrymen who was to go on to
produce many more for ballet.

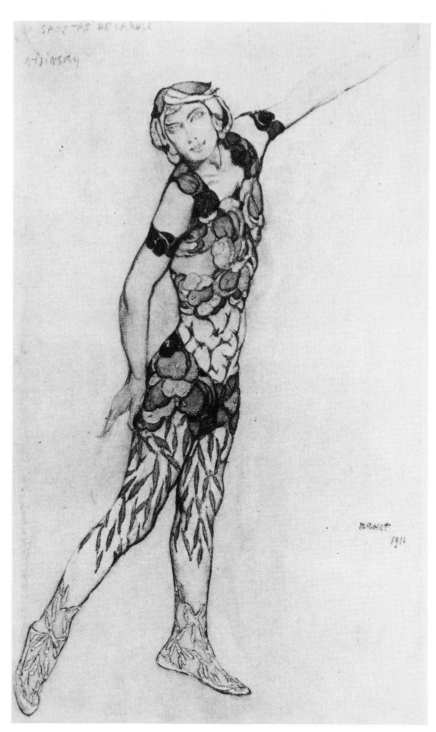

124

His legacy

During the twenty years of his company's existence Diaghilev presented an average of at least three new works every year. The most evident part of his legacy to succeeding generations is the group of ballets still being given today in substantially the same form as when created for him. Astonishingly, there are no fewer than sixteen of these—not far short of a quarter of his total repertory. To have so high a proportion of creations capable of surviving periods of four, five, six decades or more is really remarkable; it is not easy to think of any other theatrical enterprise (ballet, opera or drama) that has achieved anything like such a rate of success.

The surviving ballets represent all the main periods of the company's existence, although with a preponderance of the earlier works with which it first made its name. I have already mentioned that seven of them are by Fokine. *Les Sylphides* is done all the time by many companies, and *Le Spectre de la Rose* has so far been sure of revival whenever there are two dancers thought capable of attempting it, even though almost everyone is agreed no cast has really matched the couple for whom it was made. *Petrushka* has been shown, whenever it is given, to have an immense attraction still, and productions of *Carnaval* and *Firebird, Scheherazade* and the dances from *Prince Igor*—although less frequent now than they were up to about ten or fifteen years ago—still attract enthusiasm. An extract from *Le Pavillon d'Armide* has also been revived as an historical curiosity.

From Diaghilev's middle period comes a smaller but still representative group of surviving ballets: Nijinsky's *L'Après-midi d'un Faune* and some of Massine's comedies, *The Good-Humoured Ladies* (somewhat neglected lately), *La Boutique Fantasque* and *The Three-cornered Hat*, to which has recently been added *Parade*. If we exclude *Pulcinella*, also revived by Massine but with new choreography, there are only four works still given from Diaghilev's second decade, but these include perhaps the best of all: Nijinska's *Les Noces* and *Les Biches*, and Balanchine's *Apollo* together with (on a slightly lower level but still tremendously effective and representative of an interesting period of expressionism) *The Prodigal Son*.

Leon Bakst: drawing of Vaslav Nijinsky in *Le Spectre de la Rose*, 1911

Pablo Picasso: drawing of *Les Sylphides*, 1919

126

It is worth remembering, too, that revivals of these ballets are not given only by the big classically-based ballet companies (like the British and Danish Royal Ballets) which deliberately pursue a policy of preserving masterworks from the past; they are chosen by companies which need to make a commercial success if they are to survive (American Ballet Theatre and London Festival Ballet have been outstanding examples) and also by companies which, for the most part, pursue an experimental policy but find certain works from Diaghilev's repertory particularly suitable to add variety and background to their own: the City Center Joffrey Ballet in New York and the Scottish Ballet have both done this.

Apart from revivals, as exact as practicable, of Diaghilev's ballets in their original form, quite a few of Diaghilev's specially written scores have been used over and over for new productions. This applies especially to the Stravinsky ballets, all of which have been given occasionally, and some very frequently. *The Rite of Spring* especially has been given many new interpretations, usually preserving the original theme; *The Firebird* is produced hardly less frequently, sometimes with new scenarios. To look at pictures of different *Firebird* productions over the years (including the two completely different décors and many different variants of the Firebird's own costumes for Diaghilev himself) is to see in miniature a conspectus of changing taste and fashion in ballet. *Les Noces* and *Petrushka* have been reworked too; and among the ballets by other composers, the previously unsuccessful *Daphnis and Chloe* became, with Ashton's 1951 production for the Royal Ballet, one of that company's most precious works; while *Jeux* has also attracted a good deal of interest among choreographers and *The Legend of Joseph* has been rehabilitated in Vienna.

The death of Diaghilev seemed to stun his collaborators and (perhaps wisely) nobody tried very seriously to continue the company without him as its leader. Within a few years however there were many imitators of the policy which had proved so successful for him. The various Ballets Russes which flourished during the 1930s and 1940s under the direction of Colonel de Basil, René Blum and Serge Denham all drew from the Diaghilev repertory and presented new works devised to a similar formula with similar dancers. The way they thrived for so long showed the strength of the tradition Diaghilev and his colleagues had started; the fact that they eventually went into a decline, being unable to keep up with changing tastes, proves that the Diaghilev achievement was not just the result of a formula which could be successfully applied by others, but the outcome of an attitude which had to be fully assimilated before it could be appropriate to new circumstances.

Nor was it enough merely to follow the taste of one man, as the Marquis de Cuevas demonstrated when he formed a similarly styled company in the late 1940s; it flourished for some years because he had a good eye for dancers, but produced hardly anything of lasting value. American Ballet Theatre, although drawing on the Ballets Russes tradition fairly heavily when it began in 1940, was always more widely based and through this it succeeded in building the character of its own which is the essential characteristic of any successful ballet company. To imitate Diaghilev was not enough; the lesson of his company was the vital need to have something distinctive to offer.

So it happened that the outstanding heirs of Diaghilev were those who learned from him but did not really imitate him at all, the most important of them being Balanchine in America, Rambert and de Valois in Britain. Ninette de Valois wrote that she had joined Diaghilev's company 'with a miscellaneous set of aims and aspirations; a wish to study production, a desire to acquire a working knowledge of existing ballets, and, last but not least, to escape none too soon from the commercial theatre ... That there was a natural ambition towards promotion as a dancer goes without saying, but fate decided that, at a later date, the knowledge acquired and experience gained should be put to another purpose.' Being by nature both observant and analytical, the young Irishwoman noted the way Diaghilev developed individual dancers and showed them to best advantage; she noted the way he subordinated them as individuals, when necessary, to the continuing good of the organization as a whole. She admired his work tremendously but saw its faults too, and when she founded the small company known as the Vic-Wells Ballet which later grew into Britain's Royal Ballet, she applied what she had learned from him to the development of her own company.

Of course de Valois was affected by other influences too: it is notable, for instance, that her own ballets included new versions of two Diaghilev ballets, *Barabau* and *The Gods Go A'Begging*, but also two first created by Les Ballets Suédois, *The Jar* and *La Création du Monde*. She also drew heavily on the old, pre-Diaghilev Russian classics for her repertory. But Diaghilev seems to have been the biggest single influence in the preparation of her grand strategy, and it is quite possible that, if he had not first shown the possibility of a continuing repertory ballet company of high standards, the idea of forming such a company in Britain might never have seemed practicable. The other great instigator of British ballet, Marie Rambert, also worked for Diaghilev (as a Dalcroze pupil she was engaged to help Nijinsky follow the music of *Rite of Spring*). The company she formed had Karsavina and Woizikovsky as guests, mounted *Faune, Carnaval* and a solo from *Les Matelots*, and pursued a creative policy similar to Diaghilev's. Besides, she more than anyone else seemed to inherit Diaghilev's flair for finding and launching other choreographers.

Les Biches (Bronislava Nijinska)
Ninette de Valois

128

George Balanchine, in founding the School of American Ballet and the world-famous New York City Ballet which eventually developed from it, was certainly not consciously following Diaghilev's example in the same way as de Valois did. He looked back to the source of Diaghilev's own company, the Imperial Theatre in St Petersburg with its attached school. Yet his years with Diaghilev had developed him from a young revolutionary with romantic aspirations into the classicist who was able to found an American style of ballet, and the collaboration with Stravinsky which began under Diaghilev's auspices grew into the relationship in which, as the composer remarked, he had scarcely finished a new piece of music before Balanchine was making a ballet of it.

Although neither Anton Dolin nor Serge Lifar can be said to have achieved as much as de Valois or Balanchine, each of them has played an important part in shaping a further generation of dancers by personal example and by their leadership of the companies they directed—Lifar at the Paris Opéra, Dolin with successive private ventures. They too would readily admit how much they learned about their art from Diaghilev. They and others who had passed under Diaghilev's influence were—as dancers, producers, designers, composers, teachers—among the leaders of ballet in most countries for the next one, two, or even three or more decades after their old master's death.

And now, half a century after his work ended, Diaghilev has become a myth rather than a person. He is the symbol of what can be achieved by ballet, its power to excite and delight, its ability both to satisfy the connoisseur and to thrill large audiences. His name is a rallying cry for those who have their own solutions to offer as to what new developments are most desirable, how new talent should be encouraged, what balance should be struck between the different elements that make up the complex art he and his collaborators served so well and so long. Everybody now rebuilds Diaghilev in his own image.

Yet how misleading an impression we should have had of him if his work had ended after its first five years, or first ten, instead of continuing for twenty. And from this it is easy to deduce if Diaghilev had lived and his company had continued, it might have changed as much during the 1930s as

The Triumph of Neptune (Lord Berners)
George Balanchine

it had already done during the two previous decades. So to try to imitate his actions is dangerous, although something can still be learned from his approach. Or was even that—with its autocratic style and reliance on private patrons—something that would work for a period only, which had perhaps already outlived its time and needed to give way to the new kind of ballet company which grew up, especially in Britain and America, after his death?

Those who knew him and worked with him should have the last word. Tamara Karsavina wrote in an anniversary tribute five years after his death that 'to honour his memory only as the creator and the soul of the Ballet Russe is to appreciate him in part only. He was the anthology of the epoch remarkable for the vitality and rapid maturing of its artists, he was the sum and substance of his time.'

Mikhail Larionov:
caricature of Serge Diaghilev, about 1925
By courtesy of Sotheby & Co.

Valentin Serov: portrait of Serge Diaghilev, about 1899

And Ninette de Valois wrote (in 1937, but it still seems applicable): 'His work was done at the time he died, and the lull that followed was a valuable relaxation for all concerned. What is happening in the ballet world today may ultimately stand as a memorial to the man who succeeded in saving the ballet from itself.'

Diaghilev himself said 'Luckily there are ten people in this world who understand my work.' Even more luckily, far more than they have enjoyed, admired and emulated it, and some had their lives transformed in the process.

Opposite: Le Dieu Bleu (Michel Fokine)
Vaslav Nijinsky as the Blue God

Mikhail Larionov: drawing of Natalia Gontcharova, Serge Diaghilev, Leonide Massine and Diaghilev's servant Beppo, 'au Petit Saint-Benoit', Paris, about 1917

Productions of the Diaghilev Ballet

date of première	title	composer	choreographer	designer	author of plot or theme	principal dancers at première
19.5.1909	Le Pavillon d'Armide[1]	Tcherepnin	Fokine	Benois	Benois, after Gautier	Pavlova, Fokine, Nijinsky, Bulgakov
	Polovtsian dances (in Prince Igor)	Borodin	Fokine	Roerich	—	Bolm, Fedorova, Smirnova
	Le Festin[2]	Glinka, Tchaikovsky, Moussorgsky, Glazunov, Rimsky-Korsakoff	Petipa, Gorsky, Fokine, Goltz, Kchessinsky	scenery: Korovin costumes: Bakst, Benois, Bilibin, Korovin	—	Karsavina, Nijinsky
2.6.1909	Les Sylphides[1]	Chopin	Fokine	Benois	Fokine	Pavlova, Karsavina, Baldina, Nijinsky
	Cleopatra[3]	Arensky, Taneyev, Rimsky-Korsakoff, Glinka, Glazunov, Moussorgsky, Tcherepnin	Fokine	Bakst[4]	Fokine	Pavlova, Rubinstein, Karsavina, Fokine, Nijinsky, Bulgakov
20.5.1910	Le Carnaval[5]	Schumann	Fokine	Bakst	Fokine	Lopokova, Piltz, Leontier, Bolm
4.6.1910	Scheherazade	Rimsky-Korsakoff	Fokine	Bakst	Benois	Rubinstein, Nijinsky, Bulgakov
18.6.1910	Giselle[6]	Adam	After Coralli, Perrot and Petipa, produced by Fokine	Benois	Gautier and Saint-Georges	Karsavina, Nijinsky
25.6.1910	The Firebird	Stravinsky	Fokine	Golovin; some costumes by Bakst[7]	Fokine	Karsavina, Fokina, Fokine, Bulgakov
	Les Orientales	Glazunov, Sinding, Arensky, Grieg, Borodin	Various, including Nijinsky	Korovin	Diaghilev	Geltzer, Karsavina, Fokina, Nijinsky, Volinin, Orlov
19.4.1911	Le Spectre de la Rose	Weber	Fokine	Bakst	Vaudoyer	Karsavina, Nijinsky
26.4.1911	Narcisse	Tcherepnin	Fokine	Bakst	Bakst	Karsavina, Nijinska, Nijinsky

6.6.1911	Sadko ('au royaume sous-marin')	Rimsky-Korsakoff	Fokine	Anisfeldt	—	—
13.6.1911	Petrushka	Stravinsky	Fokine	Benois	Stravinsky and Benois	Karsavina, Nijinsky, Orlov, Cecchetti
30.11.1911	Swan Lake[1]	Tchaikovsky	Petipa and Ivanov, produced by Fokine	Korovin and Golovin[8]	Begitchev and Geltzer	Kchessinskaya, Nijinsky
13.5.1912	Le Dieu Bleu	Hahn	Fokine	Bakst	Cocteau and de Madrazo	Karsavina, Nelidova, Nijinsky
20.5.1912	Thamar	Balakirev	Fokine	Bakst	Bakst	Karsavina, Bolm
29.5.1912	L'Après-midi d'un Faune	Debussy	Nijinsky	Bakst	Nijinsky	Nelidova, Nijinsky
8.6.1912	Daphnis and Chloe	Ravel	Fokine	Bakst	Fokine	Karsavina, Nijinsky, Bolm
15.5.1913	Jeux	Debussy	Nijinsky	Bakst	Blanche	Karsavina, Schollar, Nijinsky
29.5.1913	The Rite of Spring	Stravinsky	Nijinsky	Roerich	Stravinsky and Roerich	Piltz
12.6.1913	The Tragedy of Salome	Schmidt	Romanov	Soudeikin	d'Humieres	Karsavina
16.4.1914	Papillons	Schumann	Fokine	scenery: Doboujinsky costumes: Bakst	Fokine	Karsavina, Schollar, Fokine
17.5.1914	The Legend of Joseph	R. Strauss	Fokine	scenery: Sert costumes: Bakst	von Kessler and von Hofmannsthal	Kuznetsova, Massine, Bulgakov
24.5.1914	Le Coq d'Or (opera produced as ballet)	Rimsky-Korsakoff	Fokine	Gontcharova	production devised by Benois	Karsavina, Jezierska, Bulgakov, Cecchetti, Kovalski
26.5.1914	Le Rossignol (opera with ballet)	Stravinsky	Romanov	Benois	Stravinsky after H. C. Anderson	
2.6.1914	Midas	Steinberg	Fokine	Doboujinsky	Bakst	Karsavina, Bolm, Frohman
20.12.1915	Le Soleil de Nuit	Rimsky-Korsakoff	Massine	Larionov	—	Massine, Zverev
21.8.1916	Las Meninas	Fauré	Massine	scenery: Socrate costumes: Sert	—	Sokolova, Khokhlova, Massine, Woizikovsky
25.8.1916	Kikimora	Liadov	Massine	Larionov	—	Shabelska, Idzikovsky
(?).8.1916	Sadko (new version)	Rimsky-Korsakoff	Bolm	Anisfeldt[9]	—	—

date of première	title	composer	choreographer	designer	author of plot or theme	principal dancers at première
23.10.1916	Til Eulenspiegel	R. Strauss	Nijinsky	Jones	Nijinsky	Nijinsky
12.4.1917	Fireworks	Stravinsky	None	Ballo	Production devised by Diaghilev	None
	The Good-Humoured Ladies	Scarlatti, arr. Tommasini	Massine	Bakst	Massine after Goldoni	Lopokova, Tchernicheva, Mme Cecchetti, Massine, Cecchetti, Idzikovsky, Woizikovsky
11.5.1917	Contes Russes[10]	Liadov	Massine	Larionov	—	Tchernicheva, Sokolova, Woizikovsky, Jazvinsky, Idzikovsky
18.5.1917	Parade	Satie	Massine	Picasso	Cocteau	Lopokova, Shabelska, Massine, Zverev
5.7.1919	La Boutique Fantasque	Rossini, arr. Respighi	Massine	Derain	Massine	Lopokova, Massine, Idzikovsky
22.7.1919	The Three-cornered Hat	de Falla	Massine	Picasso	Sierra after Alarcón	Karsavina, Massine, Woizikovsky
2.2.1920	Le Chant du Rossignol[11]	Stravinsky	Massine	Matisse	Stravinsky	Karsavina, Idzikovsky, Sokolova, Grigoriev
15.5.1920	Pulcinella	Stravinsky, after Pergolesi	Massine	Picasso	Massine	Karsavina, Tchernicheva, Nemchinova, Massine, Idzikovsky, Cecchetti
27.5.1920	Le Astuzie Femminili (opera-ballet)	Cimarosa	Massine	Sert	—	Karsavina, Tchernicheva, Nemchinova, Sokolova, Idzikovsky, Woizikovsky
15.12.1920	The Rite of Spring (new production)	Stravinsky	Massine	Roerich	Stravinsky and Roerich	Sokolova
17.5.1921	Chout	Prokofiev	Larionov and Slavinsky	Larionov	—	Devillier, Slavinsky, Jazvinsky
	Cuadro Flamenco	Traditional Spanish	Traditional Spanish	Picasso	—	Dalbaicin
2.11.1921	The Sleeping Princess[1]	Tchaikovsky	Petipa, produced by Sergueeff, with additions by Nijinska	Bakst	Vsevolozhsky, after Perrault	Spessivtseva, Lopokova, Brianza, Vladimirov, Idzikovsky

18.5.1922	Aurora's Wedding[12]	Tchaikovsky	Petipa and Nijinska	costumes: Benois[13] and Gontcharova	Vsevolozhsky, after Perrault	Trefilova, Vladimirov
	Le Renard	Stravinsky	Nijinska	Gontcharova	Stravinsky	Nijinska, Idzikovsky, Jazvinsky, Fedorov
13.7.1923	Les Noces	Stravinsky	Nijinska	Gontcharova	Stravinsky	Tchernicheva, Doubrovska, Semenov, Woizikovsky
3.1.1924	Les Tentations de la Bergère	Monteclair, edited Casadesus	Nijinska	Gris	—	Nemchinova, Nijinska, Tchernicheva, Woizikovsky, Vilzak
6.1.1924	Les Biches	Poulenc	Nijinska	Laurençin	—	Nemchinova, Nijinska, Vilzak
8.1.1924	Cimarosiana[14]	Cimarosa	Massine	Sert	—	Nemchinova, Tchernicheva, Sokolova, Idzikovsky, Woizikovsky, Vilzak
19.1.1924	Les Fâcheux	Auric	Nijinska	Braque	Kochno, after Molière	Tchernicheva, Vilzak, Dolin
13.4.1924	Night on the Bare Mountain	Moussorgsky	Nijinska	Gontcharova	—	Sokolova, Fedorov
20.6.1924	Le Train Bleu	Milhaud	Nijinska	scenery: Laurens costumes: Chanel curtain: Picasso	Cocteau	Dolin, Nijinska, Sokolova, Woizikovsky
28.4.1925	Zephyre et Flore	Dukelsky	Massine	Braque	Kochno	Nikitina, Dolin, Lifar
17.6.1925	Les Matelots	Auric	Massine	Pruna	Kochno	Nemchinova, Sokolova, Woizikovsky, Lifar, Slavinsky
	Le Chant du Rossignol (new production)	Stravinsky	Balanchine	Matisse	Stravinsky	Markova, Sokolova
11.12.1925	Barabau	Rieti	Balanchine	Utrillo	Rieti	Woizikovsky, Lifar, Chamie
4.5.1926	Romeo and Juliet	Lambert	Nijinska and Balanchine	Ernst and Miró	—	Karsavina, Lifar
29.5.1926	La Pastorale	Auric	Balanchine	Pruna	Kochno	Doubrovska, Danilova, Lifar, Woizikovsky

date of première	title	composer	choreographer	designer	author of plot or theme	principal dancers at première
3.7.1926	Jack-in-the-Box	Satie	Balanchine	Derain	—	Danilova, Tchernicheva, Doubrovska, Idzikovsky
3.12.1926	The Triumph of Neptune	Berners	Balanchine	Shervashidze, after Pollock prints	Sacheverell Sitwell	Danilova, Tchernicheva, Sokolova, Lifar, Balanchine
30.4.1927	La Chatte	Sauguet	Balanchine	Gabo and Pevsner	'Sobeka'[15] after Aesop	Spessivtseva, Lifar
3.5.1927	Les Fâcheux (new production)	Auric	Massine	Braque	Kochno after Molière	Massine
2.6.1927	Mercure[16]	Satie	Massine	Picasso	Cocteau	Petrova, Massine, Lissanevich
7.6.1927	Le Pas d'Acier	Prokofiev	Massine	Yakoulov	Prokofiev and Yakoulov	Tchernicheva, Danilova, Petrova, Massine, Lifar, Woizikovsky
6.6.1928	Ode	Nabokov	Massine	Tchelichev	Kochno	Doubrovska, Nikitina, Massine, Lifar
12.6.1928	Apollo	Stravinsky	Balanchine	Bauchant	—	Nikitina, Tchernicheva, Doubrovska, Lifar
16.7.1928	The Gods Go A'Begging	Handel, arr. Beecham	Balanchine	scenery: Bakst[17] costumes: Gris[18]	'Sobeka'[15]	Danilova, Woizikovsky
9.5.1929	Le Bal	Rieti	Balanchine	de Chirico	Kochno	Danilova, Dolin, Doubrovska, Woizikovsky, Balanchine, Lipkovska, Lifar
21.5.1929	Le Renard (new production)	Stravinsky	Lifar	Larionov	—	Woizikovsky, Efimoff, Hoyer, Lissanevich
	The Prodigal Son	Prokofiev	Balanchine	Rouault	Kochno	Doubrovska, Lifar, Woizikovsky, Dolin

Notes

1 New production of ballet created at the Maryinsky Theatre, St Petersburg.

2 Included (under title of *L'Oiseau de Feu*) the Bluebird *pas de deux* from *The Sleeping Beauty*, later given as a separate item under different titles. A revised version of *Le Festin*, with some different items and a changed running order, was given in 1910.

3 Revised version of ballet created under title of *Une Nuit d'Egypte* at the Maryinsky Theatre, St Petersburg.

4 New scenery by Delaunay used in 1918.

5 New production of ballet created for charity performance at Pavlov Hall, St Petersburg.

6 New production of ballet created at the Paris Opéra in 1841.

7 New designs by Gontcharova used from 1926.

8 Scenery and costumes designed for and bought from the Bolshoi Theatre, Moscow.

9 New costumes by Gontcharova used in 1918.

10 Included *Kikimora*.

11 Ballet adapted from the opera *Le Rossignol*.

12 Adapted from dances from *The Sleeping Princess*; Bakst's first act setting used in later revivals.

13 From *Le Pavillon d'Armide*.

14 Adapted from *Le Astuzie Femminili*.

15 Pseudonym of Kochno.

16 New production of ballet created for Comte Etienne de Beaumont's Soirées de Paris.

17 From *Daphnis and Chloe*.

18 From *Les Tentations de la Bergère*.

Book list

Very many books have been written about the Diaghilev era. For anyone who wants to find out more about the man, his colleagues and their period, this arbitrary selection of some of the most interesting sources may be useful. Many of them (especially the older ones) are out of print, but good libraries should be able to help. The fact that so many of the authors contradict each other on details, or even on major facts, should be a reminder to take all accounts (including the present one) with a healthy scepticism —and above all in those instances where the author was personally concerned.

Beaumont, Cyril *The Diaghilev Ballet in London—a personal record* 1940 Putnam, London; 1951 A. & C. Black, London

Benois, Alexandre *Reminiscences of the Russian Ballet* 1947 Putnam, London

Buckle, Richard *Diaghilev* 1979 Weidenfeld & Nicolson, London; Atheneum, New York

Buckle, Richard *Nijinsky* 1971 Weidenfeld & Nicolson, London

Cooper, Douglas *Picasso Theatre* 1968 Weidenfeld & Nicolson, London

De Valois, Ninette *Invitation to the Ballet* 1937 The Bodley Head, London

Dolin, Anton *Divertissement* 1931 Sampson Low, London

Dyer, Philip, and Battersby, Martin chapters in *The World of Serge Diaghilev* by Charles Spencer 1974 Paul Elek, London

Fokine, Michel *Memoirs of a Ballet Master* 1961 Little, Brown, Boston

Grigoriev, S. L. *The Diaghilev Ballet 1909–1929* 1953 Constable, London

Haskell, Arnold *Diaghilev, His Artistic and Private Life* 1935 Gollancz, London

Karsavina, Tamara *Theatre Street* 1948 Constable, London; 1961 Dutton, New York

Kirstein, Lincoln *Nijinsky Dancing* 1975 Alfred A. Knopf, New York; Thames and Hudson, London

Kochno, Boris *Le Ballet en France du quinzieme siècle à nos jours* 1954 Hachette, Paris

Kochno, Boris *Diaghilev and the Ballets Russes* 1970 Allen Lane The Penguin Press, London; Harper & Row, New York

Lievin, Prince Peter *The Birth of the Ballets-Russes* 1936 Allen & Unwin, London

Lifar, Serge *Diaghilev, An intimate Biography* 1940 Putnam, London

Lifar, Serge *Ma Vie* 1965 Juillard, Paris; translation 1970 Hutchinson, London

Macdonald, Nesta *Diaghilev Observed* 1976 Dance Horizons, New York and Dance Books, London

Magriel, Paul (editor) *Nijinsky* 1948 A. & C. Black, London

Massine, Leonide *My Life in Ballet* 1968 Macmillan, London

Nijinsky, Romola *Nijinsky* 1933 Gollancz, London

Nikitina, Alice *Nikitina, by Herself* 1959 Wingate, London

Propert, W. A. *The Russian Ballet in Western Europe, 1909–1920* 1921 The Bodley Head, London

Propert, W. A. *The Russian Ballet 1921–1929* 1931 The Bodley Head, London

Reiss, Françoise *Nijinsky* 1960 A. & C. Black, London

Roslavleva, Natalia *Era of the Russian Ballet 1770–1965* 1966 Gollancz, London

Sert, Misia *Two or Three Muses* 1953 Museum Press, London

Sokolova, Lydia *Dancing for Diaghilev* 1960 John Murray, London

Stravinsky, Igor *An Autobiography* 1936 Simon & Schuster, New York

Wolkonsky, Prince Sergei *My Reminiscences* 1925 Hutchinson, London

Index to text